M000276306

AFRICAN SANCTUS
David Fanshawe

FOR SOPRANO·SOLO, MIXED CHORUS,

INSTRUMENTAL ENSEMBLE AND PRE-RECORDED TAPE

VOCAL SCORE

FOR HIRE

Full score, instrumental parts and African tape:
The Concord Partnership, UK
Rodgers & Hammerstein Concert Library, USA
Warner/Chappell Music, Australia

FOR SALE

Miniature study score, vocal score,
African Sanctus Selections: Nos 1 & 13 Sanctus, No 2 Kyrie,
No 6 Et in Spiritum Sanctum, No 9 The Lord's Prayer (5 versions)

INTERNATIONAL RECORDINGS

1994 Silva Classics CD/Cass SILKD 6003
(definitive to the score, produced by the composer)
1987 Proprius PRCD 9984
1973 Philips 426 055-2

BBC FILM

VIDEO distributed by CTVC (CAT No: GHE 2007)
Hillside Studios, Merryhill Road, Bushey, Watford, WD2 1DR, UK

CONSULTANCY/EDUCATIONAL

Pre-Concert talks, media, photos, study packs, CD-ROM
Enquiries to Warner/Chappell, or Fanshawe direct:
Box 574, Marlborough, Wilts, SN8 2SP, UK

This edition © 2008 by Faber Music Ltd
Bloomsbury House 74–77 Great Russell Street London WC1B 3DA
First published in 1977 by Chappell Music Ltd
Printed in England by Caligraving Ltd
All rights reserved

ISBN10: 0-571-53283-7   EAN13: 978-0-571-53283-4

To buy Faber Music publications or to find out about the full range of titles available,
please contact your local music retailer or Faber Music sales enquiries:

Faber Music Ltd, Burnt Mill, Elizabeth Way, Harlow, CM20 2HX England
Tel: +44(0)1279 82 89 82   Fax: +44(0)1279 82 89 83
sales@fabermusic.com   fabermusic.com

AFRICAN SANCTUS

Scored for:

Operatic Soprano Solo
Choir (S.A.T.B.)
2 Percussion . . . . 3 or 4 Timpani
                                                Bass drum (large)
Piano   Congas (1 pair)
                                                Bongos (1 pair)
African Tape   3 Tenor drums
                                                2 Suspended cymbals
                                                Tam tam (large)
                                                Tom tom (on stand)

Optional:

Lead Guitar (amplified)
Bass Guitar (amplified)
Drum kit
Multi-racial performers ad lib
Ethnic drums, gongs & tambourine
Light/Gospel soprano solo, or children (The Lord's Prayer)
Electric organ/keyboard (The Lord's Prayer)

Note: A performance of AFRICAN SANCTUS should ideally include the optional forces, but where resources are limited the work may be performed without them. Soloist, Choir and Piano should be amplified. For further technical information - see Full Score.

Encore: This is often demanded. Repeat No 9 The Lord's Prayer (from letter A) and/or No 13 Finale and Gloria

Duration without Interval: 1 hour approximately

HISTORY and PERFORMANCE

AFRICAN SANCTUS was first performed by the Saltarello Choir in July 1972, at St John's Smith Square, London and later broadcast on BBC Radio, on United Nations Day. In 1974, BBC Television's 'Omnibus' made a documentary film about AFRICAN SANCTUS on location in North and East Africa. This film, directed by Herbert Chappell, was first screened on Easter Day, 1975 and coincided with the release of the original Philips recording. The score was first published in 1977 and live performances were premiered in Toronto, at the Three Choirs Festival in 1978 and at the Royal Albert Hall in 1979. Since then the work has gained steady momentum in the choral repertoire - literally hundreds of live performances have taken place worldwide, from Washington to Singapore, from the Sydney Opera House to South Africa. AFRICAN SANCTUS is frequently performed at Festivals, charity events, college tours; in cathedrals, churches, concert halls and outdoor venues; and selections from the work are often sung at weddings, funerals and on special occasions. It has also been choreographed. The work appears on educational syllabuses, including the International Baccalaureate. In 1994, a new definitive recording, produced by the composer, was released on Silva Classics, featuring the Bournemouth Symphony Chorus, Choristers of St George's Chapel, Windsor and soprano Wilhelmenia Fernandez. As a result of this recording, BBC TV commissioned Herbert Chappell to adapt his earlier award-winning film to the changing world of the '90s. "African Sanctus Revisited" contrasts live performance with stirring and poignant images of Africa today, giving renewed and contemporary relevance to a work that has become a landmark in our musical lives.

African Sanctus has received international acclaim.

AFRICAN SANCTUS represents Belief.

In 1969 I went to Africa for the first time with the idea of writing a major work which would combine my love of travel, adventure and recording with my composition.

On the hill of the citadel in Cairo, overlooking the Nile one evening, I suddenly heard in my head the unlikely combination of a western choir accompanying the Islamic 'Call to Prayer'. My objective at that time was to travel up the Nile to Lake Victoria, record traditional music and one day, hopefully, compose selected recordings into my own music, creating a work of Praise to One God. Armed with a stereo tape-recorder, rucksack, camera, tapes and very little else, the journey was to be achieved by hitch-hiking.

Travelling southwards I soon realised it was not going to be easy. Music permits were unobtainable. I was locked up and my equipment confiscated. When ultimately they found me innocent of spying, my first attempts at recording were most depressing - everyone seemed to own a transistor radio! In spite of initial failures however, I pressed on.

On reaching Khartoum I decided to go west, having learned about some mysterious mountains which were believed to be like 'Paradise'. Much of the time was spent on the back of a camel and on one particular moonlit night, on top of the Marra mountains, it seemed my prayers had been answered; for I happened to hear some remarkable chanting in the wilderness. I parked my camel under a 'Bird Song' tree, scrambled up the mountain as fast as I could and recorded four men sitting on a prayer mat, swaying from side to side. They were in a deep trance, perhaps on a pilgrimage to Mecca. From that moment the whole shape and purpose of my journey took on a new dimension. I decided to turn east, double back on my tracks and travel to the Red Sea.

My belief in the geographical relationship between North, West and East, followed by a lengthy expedition South into Uganda and Kenya, was to become an important symbol - The Cross. The journey became a symbolic one: a cross-shaped pilgrimage, which I like to call the 'Sanctus Journey'. As the indigenous peoples changed character from north to south, so it seemed my composition should reflect the change in their musical styles. Music composed in harmony with the Call to Prayer in Cairo, I decided, would be very different from music composed to the Acholi Bwala dance of Uganda. In many ways, the work I had in mind was a kind of musical documentary. Desert sounds, frogs, equatorial rains and thunder were all to play an important roll in communicating the atmosphere of my travels into the overall musical tapestry. An unorthodox setting of the Latin Mass was to take its final form in the shape of my travels. These were all thoughts which came to me in the wilds as I ventured towards the source of the Nile's music - Lake Victoria.

In 1970, after a brief time in England, I returned to East Africa; but it was not until the spring of 1972 that the work was actually written and entitled "African Revelations". I am indebted to Richard Bradshaw for his encouragement and to the Saltarello Choir who gave the first performance. I am also indebted to the Ralph Vaughan Williams Trust for their invaluable help and sponsorship. In 1973 I returned again, this time with my former wife, Judith, who I happened to meet on the island of Bahrain on New Year's Eve, 1970. Together we continued the search for folk music and were lucky enough to be awarded a Fellowship from the Winston Churchill Memorial Trust.

On the 19th April 1973, my 31st birthday, on the shores of Lake Victoria, we met a remarkable African of the Luo tribe named Mayinda Orawo - the 'Hippo Man'. He made a great impact on me and I decided to change the title of the work to AFRICAN SANCTUS (Holy Africa). The Hippo Man's photograph, on the front cover, represents the symbolic figurehead of all the legends and myths of Africa. At the same time, he represents Africa as it is today - a changing world and one that I want to praise in my music. Having revised the work, I recorded it with the encouragement and enthusiasm of many people who played an important part in helping it become established. Each movement is dedicated to my friends at home and abroad and I would like to thank again, in writing, especially Judith, Michael McCarthy, Alan Ferne, Sir Keith Falkner, John Lambert, Erik Smith, Teddy Holmes, Herbert Chappell, Peter Bartlett, Philip Evry, John McCarthy and the Ambrosian Singers, the conductor Owain Arwel Hughes, and Peter Olliff, our ingenious sound engineer at Phonogram Studios, London.

In November 1974 I was invited to return again to the Nile by Herbert Chappell, the composer and director, this time with a BBC film crew to retrace the places I had visited and the musicians who had inspired me. Now, finally, on completion of the full score, after eight years since its conception, I still remember that moment in time when I stood overlooking the Nile valley hoping that one day, it might be possible to hear my music on the concert platform, harmonised with the field recordings I was priviledged to find. These recordings are all extremely rare, if not unique, and I am grateful to my publishers for waiting so patiently for this hand-written manuscript which I hope will be performed on many occasions.

It has been a wonderful journey and I suppose the 'Hippo Man', Bwala Dancers, Latigo Oteng, the camel and my 'Spirit Cap', blessed by the witch doctors on the Hill of Eternity in Masailand, are all part of the secret of living and creating. That is why I sign my name and always draw a camel. In the head of the camel there is a treble clef and in the base of the camel there is a bass clef! Fanshawe is to be seen riding, somewhat precariously, on the back of the camel dreaming up music. On his head is the 'Spirit Cap' which originally came from Folkestone harbour in 1968. The camel has a long tail to tell; the desert has a palm tree and my message written in the sand is simply "I Love The World".

David Fanshawe

I Love The World

AFRICAN SANCTUS

CONTENTS

Words from the Latin Mass and Anglican Liturgy.
Recordings made by the composer in Egypt, Sudan,
Uganda and Kenya (1969-73).
The full score completed January 1977.

To Musicians who neither read nor write music.

1. AFRICAN SANCTUS

Part One

5

8

9

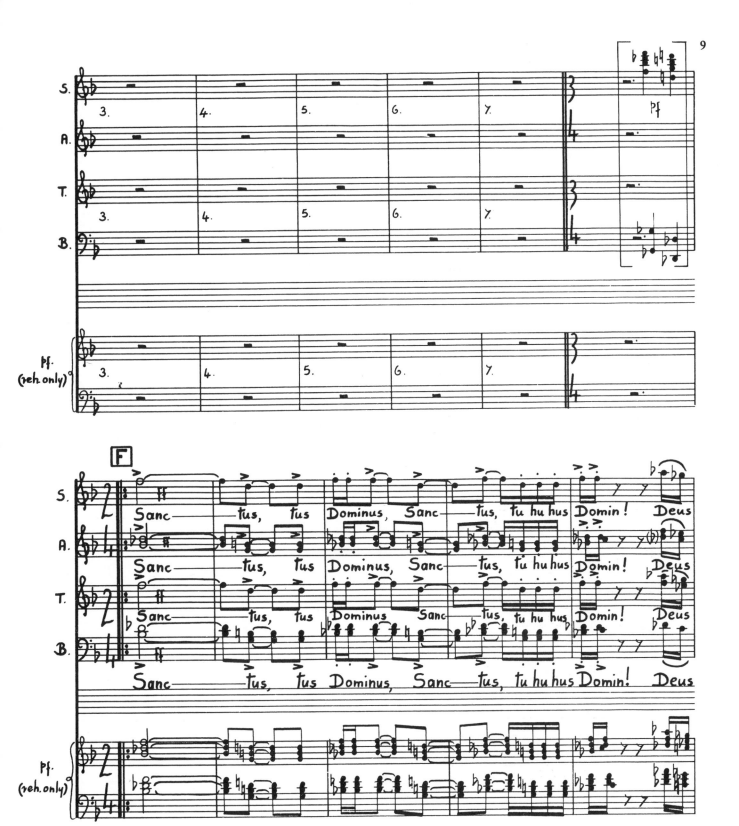

10

☆ *accapella*

To the Ambrosian Singers.
2. KYRIE: CALL TO PRAYER = #12

12

14

Hayya alal-falah. [COME HURRY TO DO THAT WHICH IS MOST NEEDFUL] Hayya alal-falah ——

— [COME HURRY TO DO THAT WHICH IS MOST NEEDFUL] ———— -lah

To Herbert Chappell.

3. GLORIA: BRIDE OF THE NILE

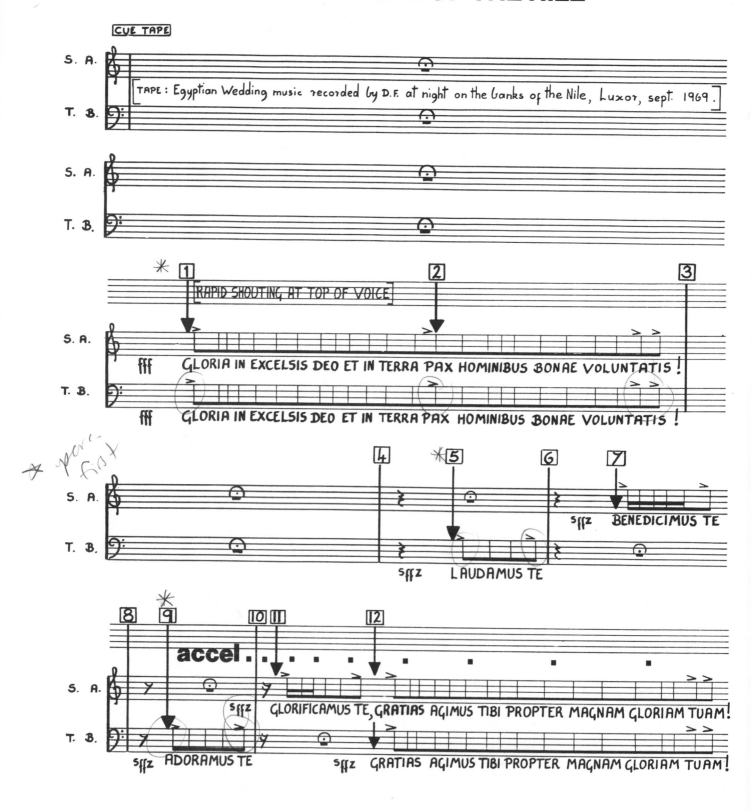

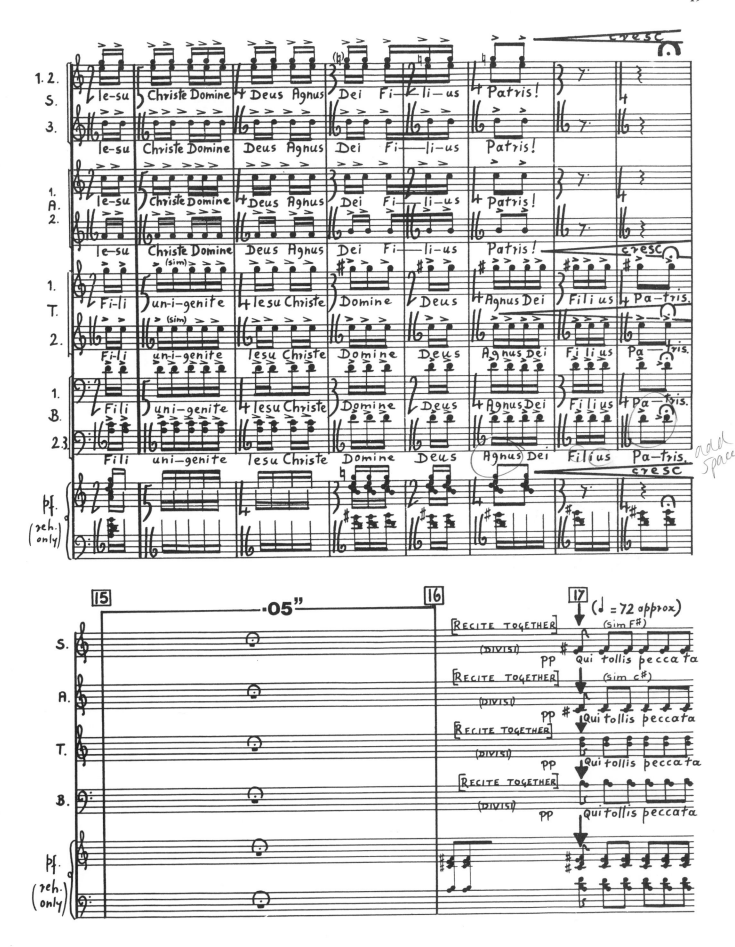

20

TAPE: Boys learn the Koran in a special Prayer School. The Gloria now juxtaposes

Latin with Arabic chanting stressing again the musical relationship between Christ and Mohammed

Islamic praye·r school

22

space,
get to note
earlier w/ body

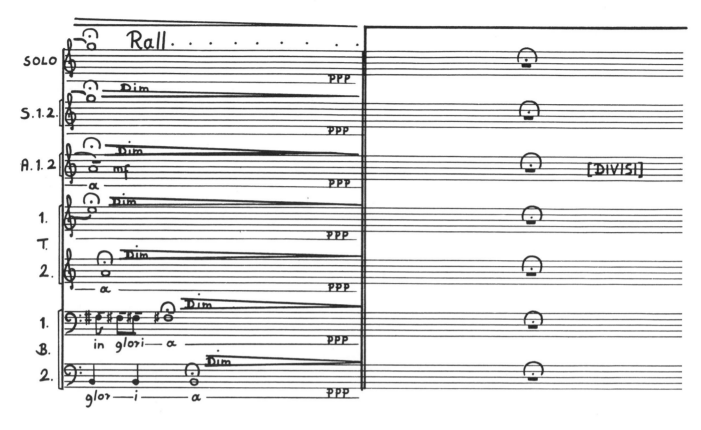

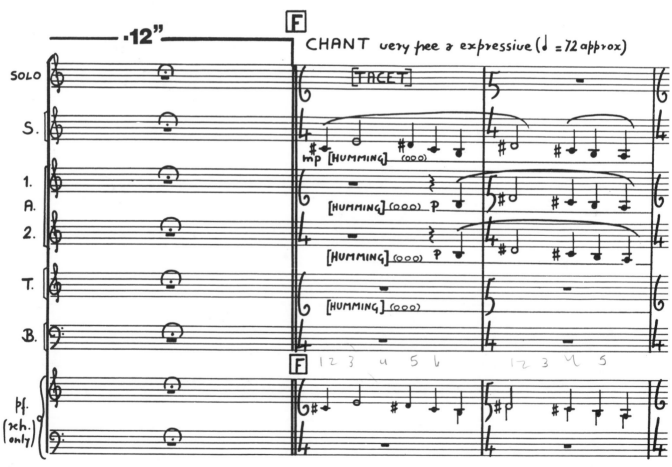

To Peter Olliff and the Four Men on the Prayer Mat.
4. CREDO: SUDANESE DANCES & RECITATIONS

30

E CREDO (tribalistic & not without humour!)

32

34

* m release

S.
A.
T.
B.
pf
(reh. only)
HOLD IT
NOTE: IF TOO HIGH SING 8VA
yumm Pa-trem omni po-ten-te m, Fac-tor
Yumm Pa-trem omni-po-ten-te m, Fac-tor
Yumm Pa-trem omni-po-ten-te m, Fac-tor
Yumm Pa-trem omni-po-ten-te m, Fac-tor
em caeli et terr-ae vis-ib-lyum om-nyumm, et in visi-bili-yu
em caeli et terr-ae vis-ib-lyum om-nyumm, et in-visi-bili-yu
em caeli et terr-ae vis-ib-lyum om-nyumm, et in-visi-bili-yu
em caeli et terr-ae visib-lyum om-nyumm, et in-visibili-yu
mm, Et in un um Domin-um le-sum Christum fili-yumm.
mm, Et in unum Domin-um le-sum Christum fili-yumm.
mm, Et in unum Domin-um le-sum Christum fili-yumm.
mm, Et in unum Domin-um le-sum Christum fili-yumm.

To my wife, Judith and Alexander our son.

5. LOVE SONG: PIANO SOLO

To Sister Maria de Fatima and Sister Majella Boyd.

6. ET IN SPIRITUM SANCTUM
I Believe in the Holy Spirit

[HOLD VOICES OVER FROGS] (as on recording PHILIPS)

End Part 1

END PART 1

Short Interval
(if desired.)

PART 2

To Latigo Oteng

7. CRUCIFIXUS: RAIN SONG

Part Two

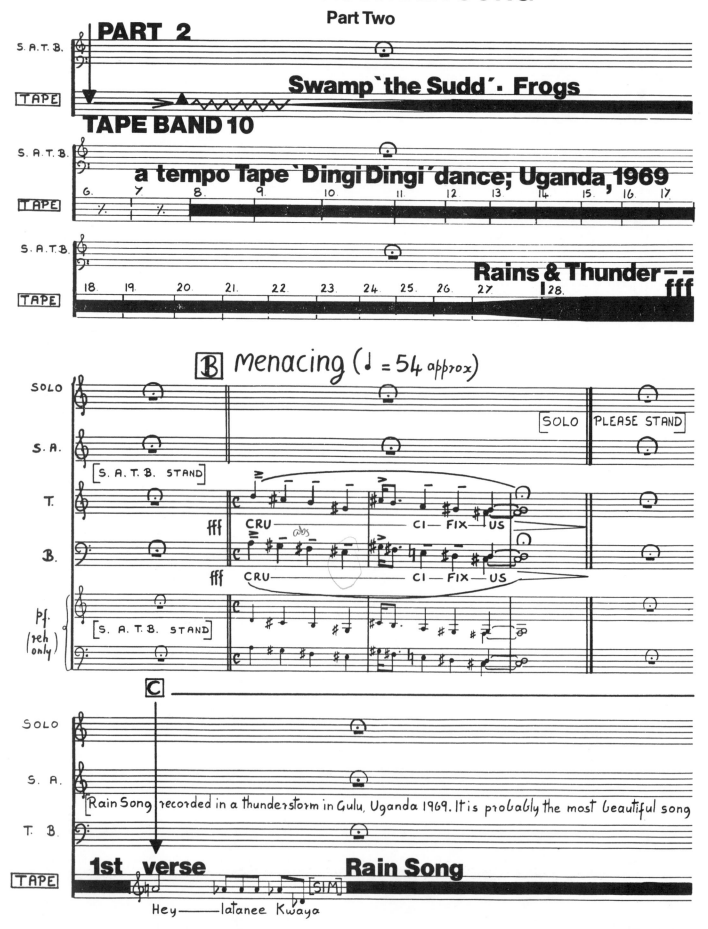

48

50

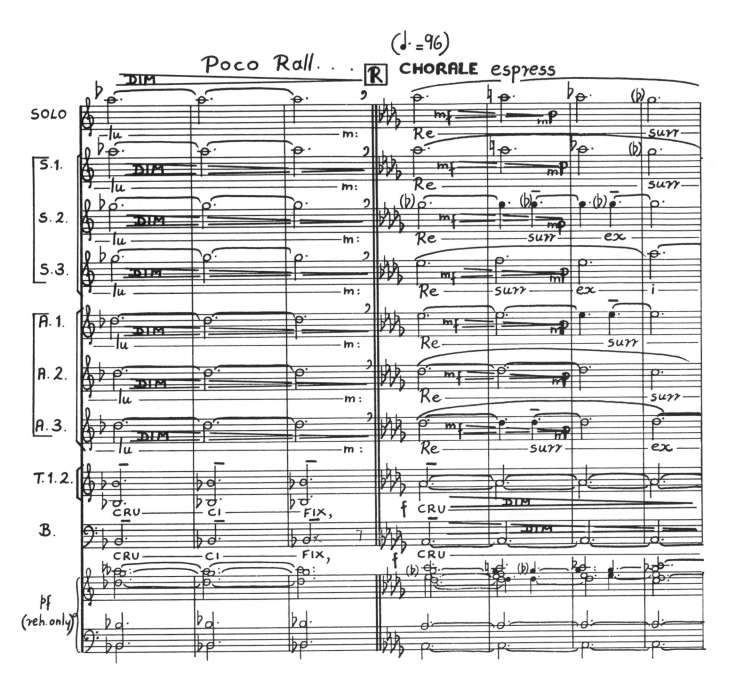

To the Acholi Bwala dancers of Uganda
8. SANCTUS: BWALA DANCE

66

70

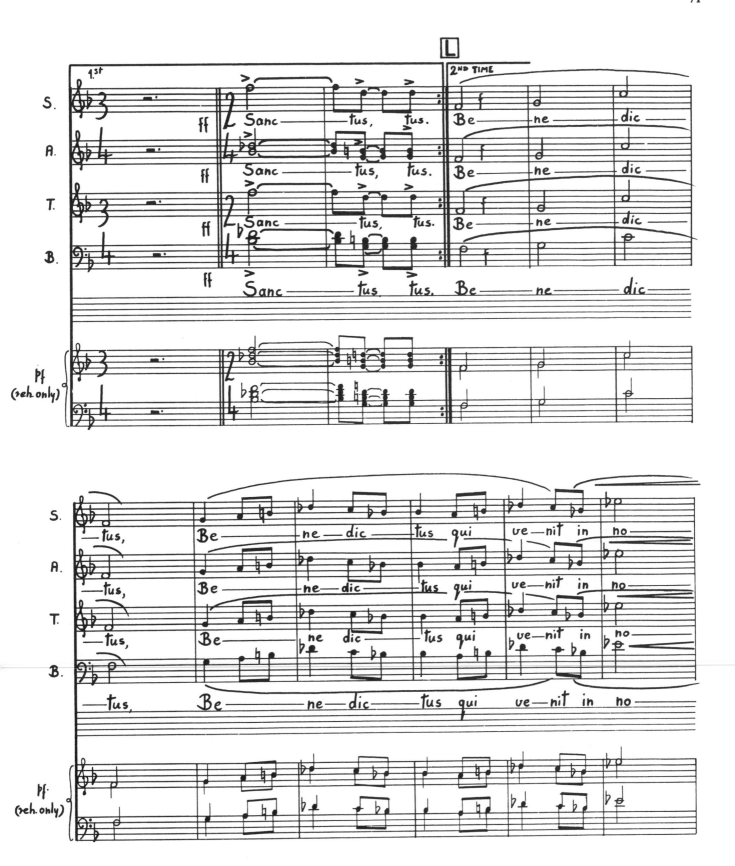

To Owain Arwel Hughes.

9. THE LORD'S PRAYER

74

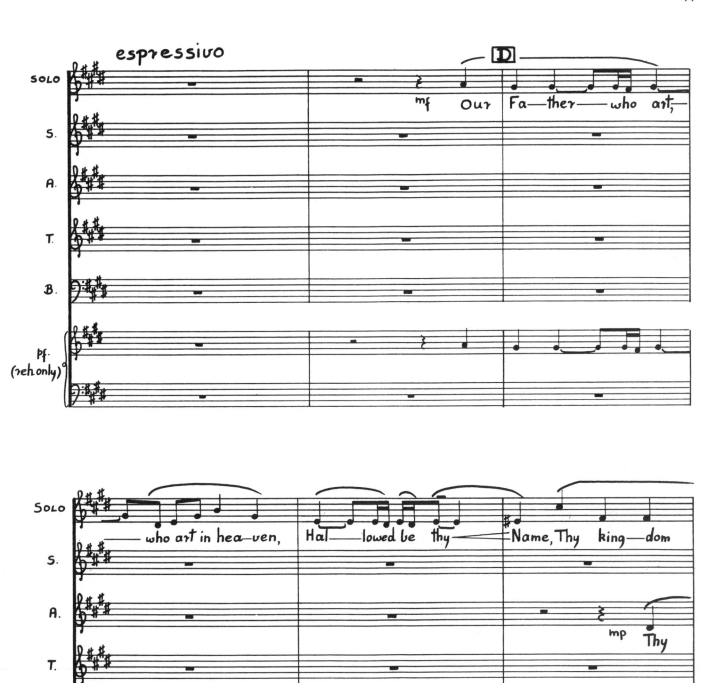

repeat 4x

Poco a Poco Rall . . .

quick page turn

To Michael McCarthy

10. CHANTS

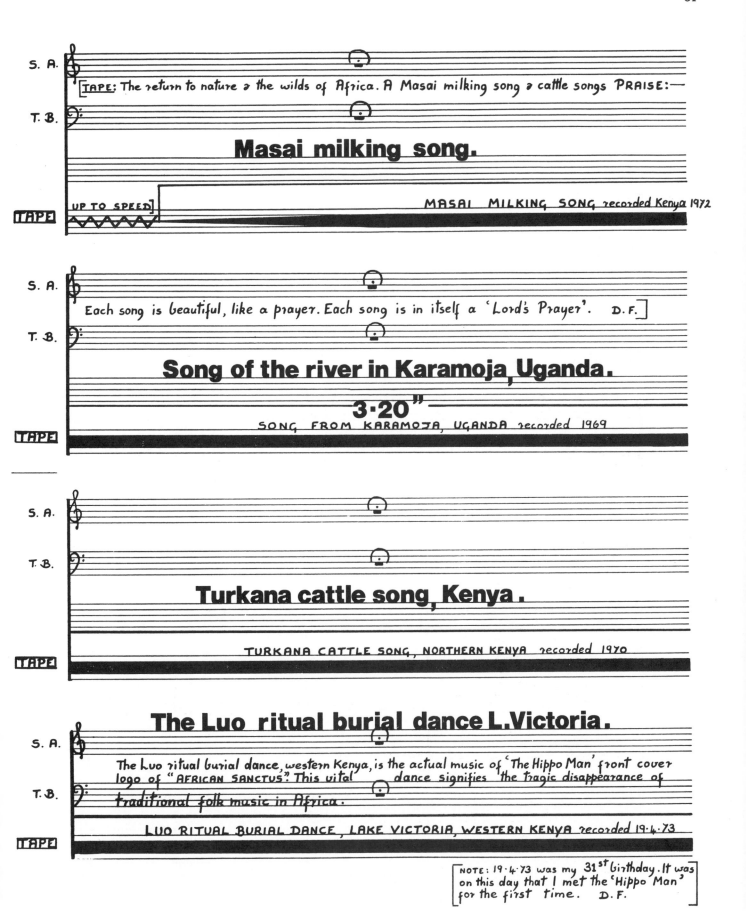

S. A.

T. B.

TAPE: The return to nature & the wilds of Africa. A Masai milking song & cattle songs PRAISE:—

Masai milking song.

UP TO SPEED

MASAI MILKING SONG, recorded Kenya 1972

TAPE

S. A.

T. B.

Each song is beautiful, like a prayer. Each song is in itself a 'Lord's Prayer'.   D. F.

Song of the river in Karamoja, Uganda.

3·20"

SONG FROM KARAMOJA, UGANDA recorded 1969

TAPE

S. A.

T. B.

Turkana cattle song, Kenya.

TURKANA CATTLE SONG, NORTHERN KENYA recorded 1970

TAPE

The Luo ritual burial dance L.Victoria.

S. A.

The Luo ritual burial dance, western Kenya, is the actual music of 'The Hippo Man' front cover logo of "AFRICAN SANCTUS". This vital   dance signifies 'the tragic disappearance of traditional folk music in Africa.

T. B.

LUO RITUAL BURIAL DANCE, LAKE VICTORIA, WESTERN KENYA recorded 19·4·73

TAPE

NOTE: 19·4·73 was my 31st birthday. It was on this day that I met the 'Hippo Man' for the first time.   D. F.

To Mayinda Orawo, my friend the 'Hippo Man'.

11. AGNUS DEI

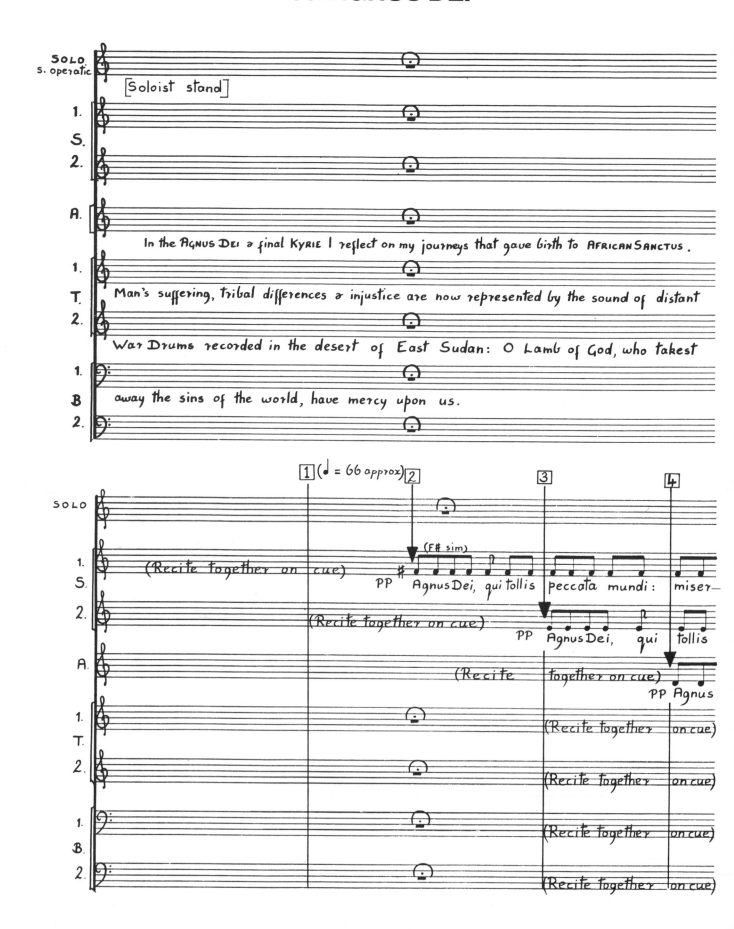

84

88

To Geoffrey Hancock.

12. CALL TO PRAYER: KYRIE

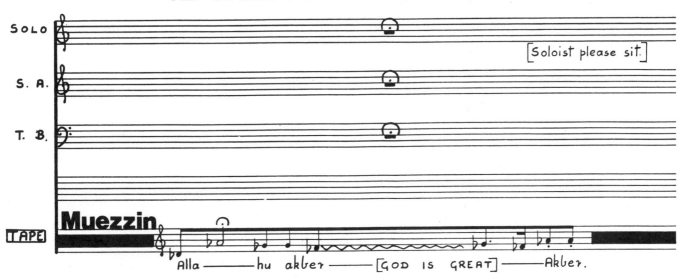

A a tempo

Tape natural fade out (OFF)

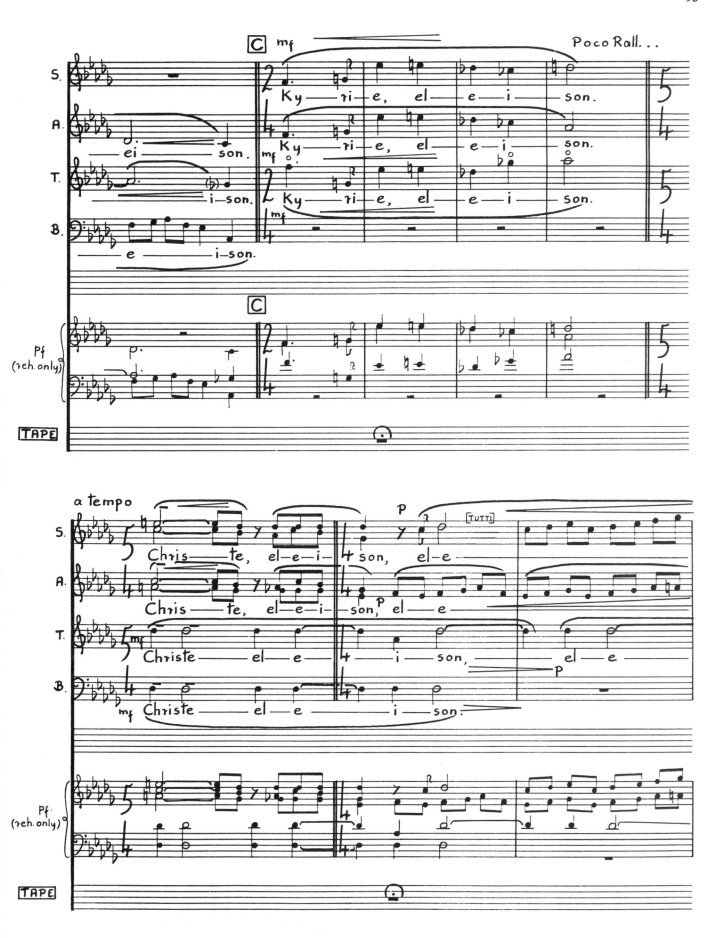

To my Family.

13. FINALE AND GLORIA

WITH POWER, RHYTHM AND EXUBERANCE ($\quarternote = 66$)

A BWALA DANCE (♩=104)

The Acholi 'Bwala', Uganda, 1969 D.F.

99

104

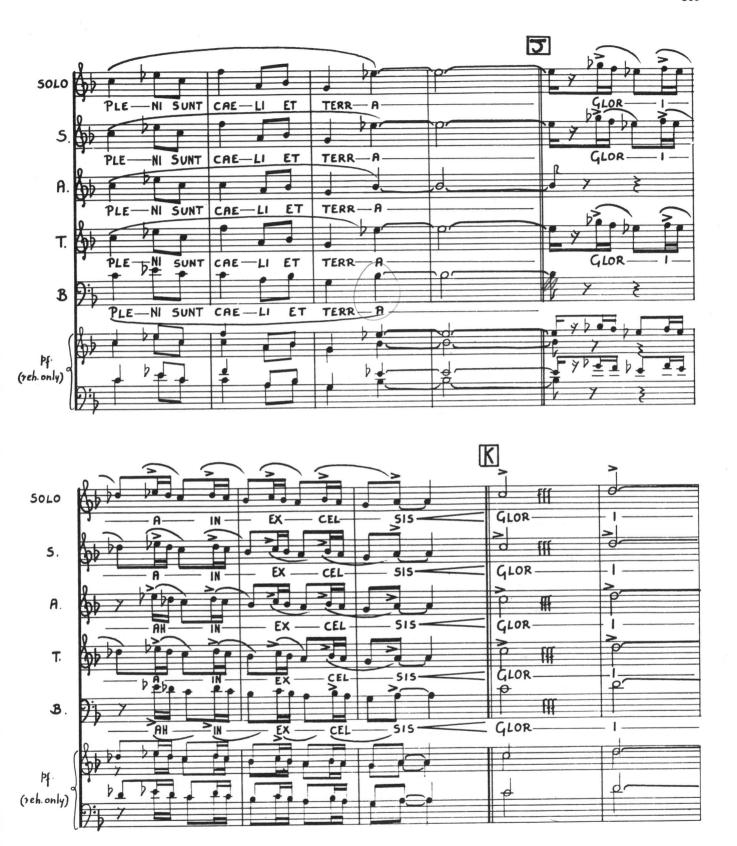

Triumphant expression

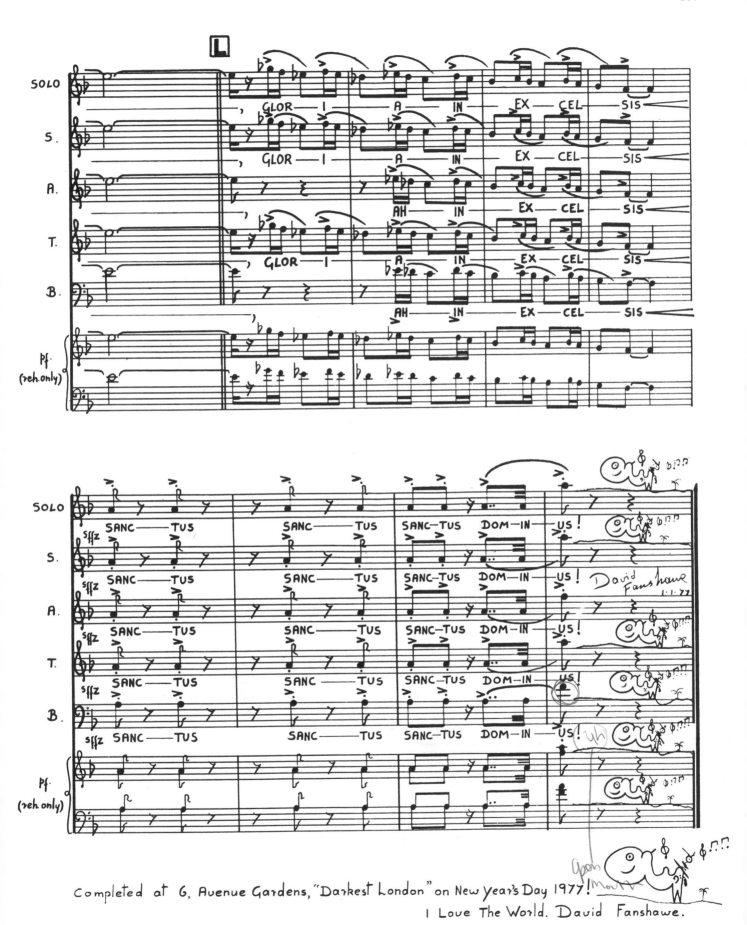

Completed at 6, Avenue Gardens, "Darkest London" on New year's Day 1977!

I Love The World. David Fanshawe.

-hx-> stage light
Print voca night live
J   Clyn